C000294401

IMAGES OF ENGLAND

Around Newent

The Market House, *c.* 1912.

IMAGES OF ENGLAND

Around Newent

Tim Ward

NONSUCH

The Quoit Ground, Newent, *c.* 1910. The site of this ground was occupied by Goulding's Transport for many years and is now part of Dennis' Plant and Contractor's yard.

First published 1994
This new pocket edition 2005
Images unchanged from first edition

Nonsuch Publishing Limited
The Mill, Brimscombe Port,
Stroud, Gloucestershire, GL5 2QG
www.nonsuch-publishing.com

British Library Cataloguing in Publication Data.
A catalogue record for this book is available from the British Library.

ISBN 1-84588-162-1

Typesetting and origination by Nonsuch Publishing Limited
Printed in Great Britain by Oaklands Book Services Limited

Contents

Introduction

Old picture postcards are based on real photographs by local photographers. They provide a fascinating and valuable contemporary source of information about ordinary people living ordinary lives whom the history books tend to neglect. Today it gives great pleasure to see such pictures and recall the old times and places they portray. They remind and recreate for us that dimly remembered and fading period that is vivid now only to our grandparents and beyond.

This book is not so much a history of Newent - the smallest town in England - as a photographic archive presenting an intimate glimpse of life in the area through the years 1890 to 1965. Most of the pictures come from my collection of postcards, which I began accumulating when we first moved to The Scarr in 1972. Since then, my collection and my knowledge of the area have grown to the point that in 1994, the centennial year of the British picture postcard, it seemed fitting to produce this book. It is a work of personal affection and local nostalgia rather than a local history.

The photographs tell us of the changes that have taken place. In 1885 the Great Western Railway's Newent Railway was opened, built on the line of the Hereford and Gloucester Canal. The railway closed in 1962 and the present bypass was built on part of it to divert traffic from the town centre. Newent had been designed to accommodate nothing larger than farm wagons, or the stage coaches which ran through Gloucester to south and mid Wales.

With today's motor traffic removed, Newent would look very much as it did in 1900. Shops have been altered and renamed, but the buildings remain largely changed. New ones have been constructed; the site of Dr Johnson's house is now the Holt's Health Centre, for example. The Onion Fair, with roundabouts, swings and 'all the fun of the fair' was held in the Market Place was only a distant memory until its recent succesful revival. The selection of photographs in this book charts these changes, good and bad, recreating for us an unknown world without cars and busy roads, where life was lived at a slower pace and where pedestrians ruled the streets.

We are indebted to the stalwart roamimg photographers of the early twentieth century for the wealth of photographic material now available to illustrate Newent's past: men such as R.H. Bisco, Marcus Martin and John Tilley of Ledbury, as well as many others who published their postcards anonymously. The quality and freshness of their work is evident throughout the book. One of them always seemed to be in the right place at the right time! Newent was also important and picturesque enough to attract the attention of the large national postcard publishers so we have cards from the vast collection of R. Tuck and Son and Francis Frith of Reigate, as well as smaller contributors such as Mr Clark from whom I have only ever seen one postcard. To all of them we owe our gratitude for the invaluable pictorial legacy they unknowingly bequeathed to us: a permanent, comforting illustration of stability and community in ever-changing modern times.

I personally owe a debt of gratitude to everyone who has helped me to produce this book, with special thanks to John Harris for allowing me to use twenty-six postcards from his collection. A list of publishers of Newent postcards is included on page 128.

I hope you will enjoy looking at the photographs as much as I have enjoyed collecting and selecting them!

Tim Ward

One

Newent from the Air

An aerial view of Newent.

W. VIEW FROM CHURCH TOWER NEWENT

Development has altered much of this 1912 view from the church tower looking towards Picklenash School with houses on the open fields beside Watery Lane, and a car park on the neat gardens in the centre. (R.H. Bisco Pub.) The message on the back reads 'Am I not living in a flat country? You can see for miles around!'

St Mary's church and Church Street from the air in 1925. Pub. Airco series 91225B. Posted 5 September 1925.

Considerable changes have taken place since this 1920 aerial view of the High Street area. The almshouses on the left disappeared about 1972 to be replaced by modern terraced town houses. Newall's Garage now occupies a large area of the upper centre of the photograph. The Holts and its beautiful garden has been replaced by the health centre and library. Pub. Airco series 91224D. Posted 7 September 1927.

Another aerial photograph clearly shows the old cattle market, now the site of the memorial hall and car park. The cattle pens are clealy visible above the Market House. Gardens and orchards have given way to modern houses. Bennion's Garage occupies much of the land beside the congregational chapel. Pub. Airco series 91224B.

Aerial view of the Culver Street area showing many small changes over the years. Pub. Airco series 91225.

Two

The Railway
and Canal

Newent station, looking towards Ledbury, *c.* 1919.

Left: The overgrown mouth of the Oxenhall tunnel twenty years after closure, c. 1905. The Herefordshire and Gloucestershire Canal Trust have cleared this area recently as part of the restoration of the canal. Pub. R.H. Bisco.

Below: Diesel railcars operated the Ledbury-Gloucester service for many years after 1940 in conjunction with steam locomotives. Here Diesel car number 19 passes the new signal box on its way to Gloucester, 9 May 1959. Pub. anon

Two super photographs of the Newent station staff about 1910. Large numbers of staff at small country stations gave passengers and local businesses excellent service, but proved to be hopelessly uneconomic when wages rose as the century progressed. This over-manning was just as much a contributory factor to the Beeching cuts as the increased use of the motor car and competition from country bus services.

Another busy view of the station twenty years after opening. Before the advent of efficient road transport, railways carried a vast amount of goods as well as passengers.

A train from Ledbury enters the station during its heyday. Note the well-kept appearance typical of the Great Western Railway. Originally called the Newent Railway when built in 1885, there were small N.R. crests on the canopy supports. Pub. I.M. Dyke, the library, Newent. Posted 1911.

Gloucester-Ledbury train arriving in Newent station. Pub. anon 23 February 1959.

The same train, loading and unloading passengers and parcels.

Amid the present debris of Newent railway station, it is still possible to see the arch in the platform where the signal and point control rods emerged from the original signal box. This view looking towards Gloucester also shows the junction with the goods yard, which for many years was busy with local produce. A replacement signal box beyond the platform, nearer the sidings was built about 1948. Pub. anon. Posted 18 June 1913.

Three

Station Street and High Street

In 1911, E. Thomas ran the New Inn in High Street, opposite the Nanfan and Dobyn Almshouses.

View from Furnace Cross up the Dymock Road in 1911. The trees have gone now, and road widening and housing development on both sides of the road have quite changed this view. Pub. Young & Co. Posted June 1911.

Dennis' Plant Hire now occupies the area on the left of the view. The Union Workhouse overlooks the railway bridge in this quiet scene where a lady with a pram could safely pose for the photographer. Pub. I.M. Dyke, the library, Newent. Posted 12 August 1918.

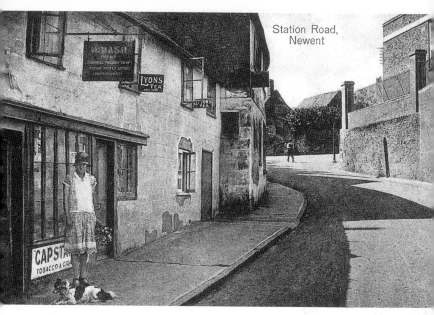

Station Road,
Newent

H. Nash's Station Supply Stores in Station Street in 1925, just after the school was built. This photograph shows how narrow the road was before these houses were demolished and the road widened as part of the bypass scheme in 1968. Pub. anon. Posted 11 September 1930.

STATION STREET, NEWENT.   21st 5-05.

Newent Union Workhouse in 1911 when Howard Trubshaw was workhouse master. It was built in 1867 for eighty inmates. Demolished *c.* 1920. The Grammar School was built on the site in 1925. Traffic lights have recently been installed on this now busy crossroads. Pub. I.M. Dyke, the Library, Newent.

Opposite above: All of these cottages in Station Street were demolished when the road was realigned during the building of the bypass. Only the bridge abutments remain beside the new fire station. The thatched cottage was the Yew Tree Inn, landlord John Baron. Anon. Photograph *c.* 1890.

Opposite below: The two houses on the left of Station Street still survive. The further one was the Anchor Inn opposite the canal company's wharf. The railings went as scrap during the Second World War. Photograph, Burrows. Pub. C.M. Bisco. Posted 21 May 1905

This scarce Second World War period postcard shows boys leaving the Grammar School. The strips of paper over the windows were to minimise flying glass caused by bomb blast. The cast-iron post has had its direction boards removed to confuse invading Germans. This policy also considerably confused British and Allied forces drivers. Above the King's Arms can just be seen the crane jib in Lancaster's Saw Mills. Note also the road markings for the 'T' junction. Pub. anon.

High Street, Newent

Another view of the school and the entrance to Newent Court. The tree-covered bank on the right was lowered for the bypass junction. A second floor was added to the school in 1957/8. Pub. anon. Posted 22 August 1933.

Left: Old Maid's Walk has changed little since this 1904 photograph. The message reads: 'I am informed that this would be more correctly named the Lover's Walk'. Pub. anon. Posted 4 June 1904.

Below: Rear view of Newent Court lodge after a heavy snowfall. This is unrecognisable now as the approach to Lakeside. Pub. anon. Posted 27 June 1915.

Two fine views of Newent Court in its heyday, overlooking the lake. It provided employment for local men and women as maids, gardeners, etc. Like many other similar country houses, upkeep proved to be too expensive as wages rose and, after a serious fire in 1942, it slowly fell into decay. Eventually it was demolished to make way for the lakeside housing development.

Numbered 2 and 3, these postcards were the first of R.H. Bisco's numbered series of at least 134.

The Wishing Bridges on the footpath to the 'White City'. These were the first council houses to be built in Newent in 1932 and are more properly known as Lancaster Terrace. This 1935 postcard was published by Pitcher, of, Gloucester.

The Wishing Bridges on the footpath to the 'White City', visible at the top of the hill, *c.* 1935. Pub. Pitcher, Gloucester.

Mantley Chase, an unusual view of the house not visible from the Ross road. Pub. anon.

A pony and trap pulls up for a chat at the top of the town. In the background is part of the old workhouse. Pub. anon. Posted August 1904.

'Snowdrop, this is the main street of a quaint place your "Blossom" is at, at this moment 5 past 12. I'm writing this in the Post Office. Andsome.' reads the message on the back of this photograph of the New Inn. Pub. R.H. Bisco No.104. Posted 1911.

High Street with a superimposed car looking out of proportion. Note the enamelled advertisement signs on W.J. Cook's bakery before the plaster was removed to reveal the timberwork. Cook's bakery is still remembered affectionately but older residents and it seems a shame it was demolished, together with the neighbouring almshouses, in 1974. Pub. A.H. Pitcher. Posted September 1910.

An anonymous postcard of the New Inn soon after it became a private house.

The bottom of the High Street in 1912. Note the white cottages where Newall's Garage now stands. The group of little children followed the photographer around the town and appear in several cards. Pub. I.M. Dyke, the library, Newent. Posted 1912.

High Street, Newent.

Mr Eves stands outside his shop on the corner of Watery Lane. Next door is the forecourt of his garage. Pub. Smith, the Wool Shop, Newent. Posted 1938.

A view down High Street in 1923 when the Devonia had become a tea room. Pub. S.A. Pitcher, College Court, Gloucester. Posted April 1923.

An attractive photograph of a traffic free High Street. The Devonia Private and Commercial Hotel was owned by Mrs Skeen and advertised accommodation for cyclists. The almshouses beside it were demolished in 1972. Pub. anon. Posted October 1920.

Newent Rectory reflects the economic changes that have occurred this century. The church has had to sell many of these huge rectories because they cost too much to maintain. At the time of writing it is for sale and redevelopment. Pub. R.H. Bisco, number 29.

Four

Lewall Street and
Broad Street

Lewall Street, 1907.

Children stop their games and errands to pose for the camera outside the parishrooms, *c.* 1912.
This card was written by a Belgian refugee in Newent in 1917. Pub. I.M. Dyke, the library, Newent.

Considerable changes have taken place in Lewall Street since this 1907 scene. The wall on the left has been demolished to make space for the wider road outside the new library and the Holt's Health Centre. Pub. R.H. Bisco, number 10. Posted 18 September 1907.

A superb photograph of the back of the Holt, Dr Johnsone's old house on the corner of Watery Lane and Lewall Street. This is now the site of the new health centre. The Holts is affectionately remembered by older residents for the garden parties and fêtes held on its spacious grounds. Pub. W.G. Coles, Gloucester. Posted 11 June 1910.

The cemetery in Watery Lane dates from 1863, when it cost £1,300 for two acres and the lodge house. This tranquil scene is now altered by the traffic to the comprehensive school opposite. Pub. anon.

Another view down a deserted Broad Street. In a similar view today the street would be crammed full of cars.

A busy scene in Broad Street in 1907. J. Bisco owned the post office on the left, now part of Bennion's Garage. The house next door disappeared about 1976 when the garage was enlarged. Pub. R.H. Bisco, number 1.

'To let you see what the main road is like! On left, where marked, is the Cong. church where we have morning assembly and IVb use the Sunday School behind. On the opposite side, round bend is the parish room where we have 3a & 3b. About 8 mins. walk further up is the Grammar School where are the 2nd form, 5b, and VI forms. Out of picture, going other way is the Women's Institute where 4A are housed & where girls have lunch. Half the school don't come in at all & we never see them.' This undated and unaddressed postcard was presumably posted in 1939 or 1940. It is thought to be from a member of staff from the evacuated Lozell's Street School, Birmingham. Information regarding evacuees is scant and information would be welcomed.

A view up an empty Broad Street in 1904. Pub. C.M. Bisco. Posted 5 May 1904.

A superb photograph from an upstairs window of the Nags Head Inn (now Barclays Bank). The view is of the local school girls in the 1911 coronation procession up Broad Street. Pub. Martin, number 2. Posted 6 September 1911.

Newent has been famous for its wild daffodils for many years. Here school children collect bunches to send to London to brighten dull hospital wards. According to an article in the Ross Gazette in April 1934 the Newent Daffodils for Hospitals scheme was started by W.H.E. Mockford, the president of the Comrades Club in 1925. Three hundred bunches wre sent to London annually via the Great Western Railway, who made special arrangements to ger them there in the best possible condition. A similar scheme operated in North Herefordshire supplying Birmingham hospitals. This anonymous card was dated 11 April 1930. Pub. anon.

The Nags Head on the corner of Culver Street has now become a branch of Barclays Bank. Berkley's, on the left, were watchmakers and jewellers for many years. Note the unmade roads before the days of surface dressing with tarmac. Pub. anon. Posted 5 October 1908.

BROAD STREET LOOKING EAST, NEWENT.

Approximately thirty years separate these two postcards and well illustrate their value as historical records. Horse transport has been replaced by motor cars and vans. Hemmings had a large grocery on the left. Note the tree outside Lloyds Bank has been removed and an overhanging sign appears for the Red Lion Hotel in the later view. Top, Pub. anon. Posted 24 September 1906. Bottom, Pub. Raphael Tuck & Sons. *c.* 1937.

A girl delivering milk poses for the camera near R.T. Smith & Co. delivery cart in Broad Street, c. 1909. Smith's were agents for the Great Western Railway Company, collecting and delivering goods in the Newent area. The railway company later took over this delivery role. Pub. anon.

The Ancient Order of Foresters, Robin Hood branch, leads a procession through the town on fête day, *c.* 1909. Pub. R.H. Bisco, number 18.

Newent Women's Institute occupied the old Nags Head on the corner of Culver Street in this 1932 postcard. John Deane had the greengrocers shop next door. Pub. anon. Posted 14 May 1932.

An excellent photograph of a deserted Broad Street in 1912. Penwarden the grocery shop displays some fine enamel signs on the side wall. The message on the back of this postcard reads: 'May 9, 1912. Madam, W. Powell begs to inform you that he will attend on Monday morning by 9 o'clock to sweep chimneys. Yours Truly, W. Powell.' Addressed to: The Housekeeper, Kempley Vicarage, Dymock, Gloshire. Pub. Young & Co.

Newent Town Band leads the local company of the Gloucestershire Regiment on their annual church parade, accompanied by a large contingent of friends and relations, c. 1905. Note also the wooden shutters on Penwarden's shop. Pub. R.H. Bisco.

Bus ADG 552 awaits passengers for Gloucester by the Corner Shop, *c.* 1918. Pub. S.A. Pitcher.

Mr Penwarden poses with his staff outside his premises in 1906 after an impressive repainting and refurbishment. Pub. anon. Posted 3 October 1906.

A winter view of Penwarden's old shop before the refurbishment. Pub. anon. Posted 13 January 1906.

Broad Street, c. 1958. The fish and chip shop now shows its familiar black and white timber. Bus stops are visible outside Barclays Banks and C.W. Hulme, the grocer. Pub. M.P. Bendle.

Ten staff pose outside the International Stores in Broad Street, c. 1930. The delivery motor cycle proclaims International Stores Newent round the rim of the front mudguard. Pub. anon.

Cars and pony traps had no difficulty parking in Broad Street near the Red Lion, c. 1930. Pub. W.H. Bendle, the library, Newent.

Five

The Market Square
and Culver Street

A busy market scene around the Market House. Fire Brigade Station says the notice over the gates, explaining why the ground area was boarded at this period. Henry Davies was the superintendant in 1910, in charge of a manual fire engine and eight volunteer firemen. Pub. R.H. Bisco, number 6.

A Victorian photograph of a group beside the Market House before the ground floor was boarded in. Pub. Tilley & Son, Ledbury.

These two postcards were issued about thirty years apart. The top view, c. 1905; the bottom view 1935. The square in the bottom right corner of the top photograph was a small weighbridge used on market days. Thirty years later one set of stairs and the weighbridge have gone. The boards around the base have been removed and an ugly telephone pole has arrived. Top picture Pub. O. S. Bidmead. Posted June 1911. Bottom picture Pub. anon. Posted 11 September 1935.

Market House, Newent.

INSPECTION OF HORSES FOR THE WAR OFFICE, AT NEWENT. AUG 5TH 14
MARTIN PHOTO

The outbreak of war on 4 August 1914 very soon affected Newent. On 5 August War Office vetinerary surgeons examined horses to be used in the war. Huge numbers of horses were requisitioned for transport in France and the Middle East but very few returned. Pub. M. Martin.

No 2   MARTIN PHOTO.

A tree-planting ceremony at the top of the market square was attended by a large crowd, while the local policeman guards the tree. Note the public convenience beside the poster covered market wall. Pub. M. Martin, numbers 5 and 6.

Newent livestock market was held fortnightly on Tuesdays. This busy scene of c.1925 has given way to the pressures of the twentieth century and has now become part of the Memorial Hall car park. Pub. by RAPCO for W.H. Bendle, the library, Newent.

Market Square, Newent

The Market Square, c. 1910.

A quiet scene in Culver Street, c. 1918. Pub. I.M. Dyke.

VIEW NEAR SOUTHENDS LANE, NEWENT.

Most of the elm trees have gone from this view of c. 1910 and the modern houses now give the top end of Culver Street a very different appearance. Pub. I.M. Dyke.

Southends Lane, 1920. As with the picture opposite, this area has been greatly changed by the passage of time. Pub. I.M. Dyke.

Conigree Court, the scene of a skirmish in the civil war. Pub. anon.

Six

Church Street

Church Street, 1910

'MINER'S STRIKE MEANS YOUR POVERTY' proclaims the Daily Mail placard outside T.A. Nealon's bakery in this 1921 view. Pub. anon.

PARDOE

FOR
DRAPERY,
MILLINERY,
MANTLES,
UNDERCLOTHING,
LINOLEUMS,
CARPETS,
MATTINGS,
RUGS & MATS,
BOOTS & SHOES,
HOSIERY,
CLOTHING,
UNDERTAKER.

Church St
Newen

Cornelius Thurston owned the large stores on the right of Church Street; he also owned the assembly rooms in Culver Street which seated 400 and later became a cinema for a time. T.A. Nealon owned the bakery and tea rooms opposite and Thomas Pardoe owned the drapers and clothiers shop next door. Pub. R.H. Bisco, number 3, c. 1908.

No longer can you pose for a photograph in the middle of Church Street as you could in 1910. Pub. I.M. Dyke.

Right: Number 2 Church Street, 1906, when it was a private house. It is now a solicitor's office. Pub. anon. Posted 3 March 1906.

Below: The George Hotel was originally a coaching inn on the post road to south Wales and has scarcely changed in appearance over the years. This 1910 advertisement card by Percy Lodge the landlord shows his business acumen in having cars for hire, the telephone (number 3), and the use of postcards to promote his business. Pub. P.C. Lodge. Printed by E.J. Burrows & Co., Cheltenham.

OLD COURT NEWENT.

Old Court as it appeared in 1910. It is now a restaurant. Pub. R.H. Bisco.

A bull-nosed Morris Oxford is parked in Church Street opposite Pardoe's successor's, H. Bray & Co. in this late 1920s view. Radermacher, Aldous & Co. printed this for W.H. Bendle, the Library, Newent to publish.

'Newent, a regular slow old fashioned place' says the message on the back of this postcard, which is also an apt description of this 1910 view of Church Street outside the church. Pub. R.H. Bisco, number 60.

A deserted street scene of Church Street, *c.* 1905. Pub. C.M. Bisco.

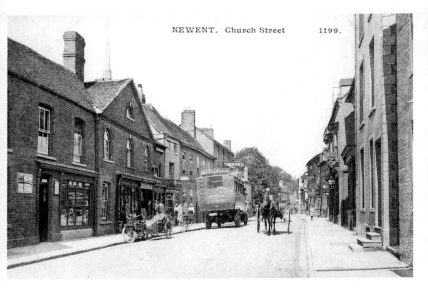

Davis & Sons bus waits for passengers in Church Street, *c.* 1925. Pub. Sydney Pitcher, Gloucester.

Church Street looking west in the winter sunshine 1912. Pub. I.M. Dyke, posted 23 September 1914.

CHURCH ST., NEWENT.

The local photographer attracted a group of interested children in Church Street and created quite a distraction on a cold winter's day. Pub. I.M. Dyke. Posted 6 January 1914.

Right; St. Mary's Church. Although this postcard view is badly damaged, it is included in the book as the only example of Mr Clark's work I have seen. Pub. Clark. Posted 6 March 1913.

Below: The Crofts. This quiet tree-lined walk bears no resemblance to the present scene. Pub. R.H. Bisco, number 31.

A large crowd of Newent people attended the unveiling ceremony outside St. Mary's Church on 3 November 1920 of the memorial to the men who died in the First World War. This is one of a set of six postcards jointly issued by M. Martin and R.H. Bisco.

An interested crowd watches Mr C.W. Bell lay the foundation stone of the Andrew Knowles Memorial, 30 May 1912. Pub. M.M. Martin.

Right: A Saxon cross shaft discovered in the churchyard in 1907. Pub. R.H. Bisco.

Below: An Edwardian view of the interior of St.Mary's Church before the gallery was removed in 1912. Pub. A. Pitcher, Gloucester.

Newent Church.

GLOUCESTER CO-OPERATIVE AND INDUSTRIAL SOCIETY LTD.

OUR LATEST VENTURE.

No. 17 Store, Newent. Opened by President, Mr. A. Burlton, April 18th, 1914.

Commemorative card for the opening of the number 17 branch, Newent, of the Gloucester Co-operative and Industrial Society on 4 April 1914 with a pictorial graph of its fifty-four year history on the back, below. This is another business that has succumbed to the harsh economics of the twentieth century. In 2004, it was demolished to wake way for more housing.

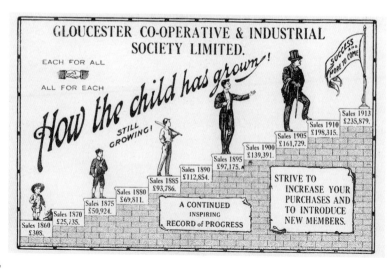

1920 view of the Co-operative Stores. The blinds proclaim:

'WE CAN SUPPLY
YOUR WANTS',

'CO-OPERATION
THE HOPE OF
THE WORKER',

'PROFITS
RETURNED
TO
PURCHASERS'.

Note the posters on the opposite wall, now demolished to make way for the Black Dog car park.
Pub. anon.

A superbly animated photograph of Church Street looking towards Town Farm House from the Co-op. Now all of these houses on the left have been demolished to make room for modern houses. The Black Dog car park occupies the area on the right. Pub. anon.

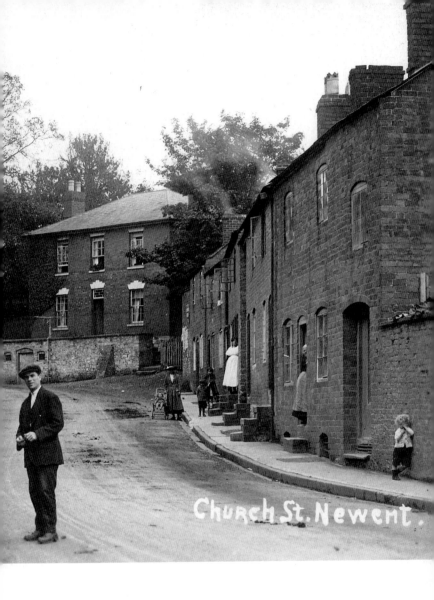

Church St. Newent.

Gloucester Road and Gloucester Terrace in Edwardian times are now only recognisable by the raised pavement and railings which escaped the demolition bulldozers of the 1970s. Pub. R.H. Bisco, number 109. Posted 22 December 1912.

This 1911 view of Gloucester Terrace looking west demonstrates the changing scene in Newent. A modern housing development has replaced the old cottages on the right. Pub. Young & Co. Posted 29 August 1911.

Seven

Newent People

Gamekeepers, at Four Oaks.

Posted on Christmas Day 1911, this is a delightful study of the meet of the Ledbury Harriers at the Scarr Farm while the Smith family were the owners. In 1933 the Land Settlement Association bought this farm and other land in the area to set up an estate for out-of-work miners and steel workers to start smallholdings and to market their produce co-operatively. For nearly fifty years this brought wealth and employment to the local economy. The manager lived in this handsome house. Pub. M.R. Martin.

An outing from Newent to Cheddar in a solid-wheeled charabanc, c. 1920. Note the speed limit of 12 mph; on this basis the round trip must have taken at least ten hours not counting on stops.

Newent Association Football Club. Proud winners of the Staunton and District Cup, 1920/21 season. Pub. M. Martin.

Newent Cricket Club and supporters 1907. The original of this photograph is extremely faded. Pub. anon. Posted 5 May 1908.

Newent Town brass band, *c.* 1914. Pub. anon.

Newent comrades minstrel troupe, 1923. Pub. anon.

Empire Day celebrations at Picklenash School Infants, 1912, at a time when Great Britain ruled the largest empire in the world. Pub. M. Martin.

A happy group of children at the school, c. 1956.

A classroom scene in Picklenash School, 1927. Pub. anon.

Newent Choral Society in *HMS Pinafore*. A picture from the *Gloucester Journal* of December 1925.

Gamekeepers pause from their summer task of tending pheasant chicks to pose outside their sheds at Four Oaks. The message on the back states that this card was sent 10 August 1908.

GROWN WITH,
HADFIELDS
SPECIAL POTATO
MANURE BY
J.H. LODGE
NEWENT · GLOS.

Mr. LODGE says—I am very pleased with results obtained with your Special Potato Manure. I weighed out equal to 17½ tons per acre and got Mr. Chew to confirm my weight, which turned out correct. This is remarkable for such a bad season, and the Potatoes were of good quality and size, many weighing 2 lb. each.

J.H. Lodge and two of his workmen pose with their record crop of potatoes. This is one of a large series of advertising postcards produced by Hadfields of Liverpool to promote their fertilisers. Pub. Hadfields. Posted 18 December 1908.

'His noble lordship, Geo. Phillips who is at the end of the tree, has joined Kitchener's army &
is ever so smart & upright now, also J. England has two stripes & is looking ten years younger,
it is the better food & no drink'. . . . reads the message on the back of this photograph of H.
Lancaster's Garratt steam engine BH894 pulling a huge tree along Ross Road opposite the saw
mills. Pub. anon.

Five men carting hay on Hunt's fields. One man and a tractor now do the job in less than half
the time. Note the fine elm trees in the background. The Dutch elm disease epidemic of 1976–
78 destroyed virtually all standing elms in Gloucestershire. The root network has now resulted
in many new trees growing, but these are still periodically attacked and suffer the virulent effects
of the beetles.

Eight

Dymock

Castle Tump. The origin is unknown, but could be a burial ground. It is certainly man-made and of great antiquity

Hill Grove, Dymock, c. 1908.

A busy scene on Dymock Station viewed from the road bridge. Between the years 1798 and 1881 the Herefordshire and Gloucestershire Canal flowed through this site, to be replaced in 1884 by the Great Western Railway's Gloucester to Ledbury branch. Pub. anon. Posted 1916.

An Edwardian view from the station towards St. Mary's church.

Another view of the station looking north in Edwardian times. The station buildings on the right were demolished in the 1960s and are now the site of Western Way old people's home. Only a section of platform by a garden remains to give a clue that this was once a busy station through which most of the trade of the local villages passed. Pub. anon.

A photograph of the old canal about twenty years after closure. By this time reeds were already growing in the cut and bushes obstructed the towpath. The Norman church stands in the background. Although Norman in origin, most of the church was rebuilt in later medieval times and the tower is early fifteenth-century. Pub. anon. Posted 22 August 1907.

A trip from Cheltenham to Dymock to see the daffodils, 4 April 1925.

The ladies of the Thackwell family at Wilton Place pose elegantly for Marcus Martin, the photographer, while the gardeners pause from hoeing the flower beds to watch, c. 1910. Note the ornate conservatory used here as a greenhouse. Wilton Place was formerly called 'the Farm'. It was sold in 1947 and broken up into flats. Pub. M. Martin.

Seven workers pose with a herd of Hereford cattle for a photograph at Pitt House Farm, c. 1908. Hereford cattle are all polled now. Pub. Tilley.

Another Edwardian view in the centre of the village with Jennings' stores on the right and the post office on the left of the street.

A horse and cart plod past the old cruck cottage, c. 1905 on this Tilley's card.

The Old Nail Shop at Greenway Cross, the home of the Saddler family, the local nailers. W.W. Gibson, the poet, lived here for a time.

Boyce Court, the home of the Deane-Drummond family. The Georgian house was built by the family on the site of a late sixteenth-century hunting lodge. The house was sold by Lieut. Col. J. Deane-Drummond to Mr Goulding in 1935.

A well-dressed group of men pose on a superb horse-drawn charabanc outside the Beauchamp Arms, *c.* 1910.

Dymock Football Club in 1912.

All the traditional fun of the fair entertained this elegant crowd at Dymock Flower Show, 26 August 1909. Pub. Tilley.

Nine

Redmarley D'Abitot

A view of Redmarley, c. 1912.

MEET OF THE LEDBURY BEAGLES AT PEYFORD BRIDGE.
FEB. 19TH 14. MARTIN. PHOTO. NEWENT No. 1.

Everyone turned to face the camera when the Ledbury Beagles met at Peyford Bridge, 19 February 1914. Pub. Martin. Posted 24 March 1914.

PELL GROVE, REDMARLEY.

Now called Pell Mell, this house has been considerably altered and enlarged since this 1914 photograph. Pub. anon. Posted 4 October 1914.

A quiet view of Redmarley Street, *c.* 1912. The Post Office was in the house on the right, now Church House. Although the village was in Worcestershire until 1932, when boundary commission changes resulted in it being incorporated into Gloucestershire, the post was routed through Newent.

Redmarley village near the crossroads, *c.* 1920. These somewhat dilapidated cottages have now been handsomely renovated. Pub. anon.

Redmarley Post Office and stores, photographed 22 June 1904. Pub. R.H. Bisco. Alfred W.S. Tozer was post master here for many years.

Memorial CROSS, REDMARLEY — shewing Union Jack) Dedication Day 10/7/20

Left: The dedication of the memorial cross on 19 July 1920 to the Redmarley men who died in the First World War. Pub. anon.

Below: The rector's family and servants pose outside the rectory in 1909. Pub. anon. Posted 1909.

REDMARLEY RECTORY.

Not to be outdone by his elders, this little boy took part in the 1909 opening meet of the Ledbury Hounds at the Down House on his toy horse no bigger than the foxhounds beside him! Pub. Tilley, number 3519.

Pleyley Corner in Edwardian times. The thatched cottage on the right has now been replaced by a modern shop and post office. Pub. W. Tozer.

Views in Redmarley village. For years Marcus M. Martin the postman, walked from Newent to Redmarley every day delivering the mail, collected the afternoon post and walked back. In his spare time he was an excellent photographer of sports groups, weddings, street scenes and the like. He produced these Redmarley postcards for Alfred W.S. Tozer, the Redmarley postmaster, to sell in his shop at 2d. each.

Not a car in sight on the Ledbury Road in this 1910 photograph. Pub. Jones, Gloucester.

A busier scene at Pleyley Corner in the 1920s. The thatched cottage on the right has now been replaced by a modern shop and post office. Pub. anon.

The landlord, R. James and his family pose outside the Rose and Crown for their own Christmas card, c. 1910.

Ten

Clifford's Mesne
and Gorsley

A group photograph somewhere in Clifford's Mesne. The photograph is rather enigmatic as the names on the back are: Marie, Celine, Victor, Madame Vauline, Franz, Josèphine and Gaston Bollansér.

Two pictures of Clifford Manor, c. 1912, when it belonged to J. Glasson. Built in 1882, it has had a chequered history since those more gracious days. For a time it was a nudist colony and is now divided into flats. Pub. R.H. Biscoe numbers 95 and 96. Posted 1913.

St. Peter's in the distance with the quarry on the right, now the site of an attractive house. Taken looking towards Kent's Green. Pub. anon.

The roadman holds some grass on his fork for the donkey while the photographer takes his picture. The village school was on the left; it is now used as a village hall. Pub. anon.

A view from the top of the old quarry. The derelict chimney served a lime kiln.
Pub. Stephens, Tibberton.

St. Peter's church, Clifford's Mesne. Built by E.S. Harris in 1882 at a cost of £1,100. Pub. anon.

A meet of the local fox hounds at the Kilcot Inn, March 1920. The fences have now been removed to give more parking. Pub. anon.

Another view of Clifford's Mesne from the top of the quarry. Pub. Stephens, Tibberton.

The front of Gorsley Goffs school is little changed in the sixty years since this photograph was taken. Extra classrooms have been built at the back to accommodate the children. Pub. Lilywhite. Posted 24 April 1935.

KILCOT NEW BAPTIST CHURCH, NEAR GORSLEY, NEWENT, GLOS.

TO BE OPENED BY H. E. WOOD, ESQ., J.P., C.C., Vice President Baptist Union, ON SUNDAY, 28th OCT., 1934, at 3.30 & 6.30, and MONDAY, 29th OCT., 3.45. Tea 5, Meeting 6.30

The Kilcot New Baptist Church was opened in 1934. This plain and uninspiring building is now redundant and has been offered for sale.

Eleven

Staunton and Corse

Staunton Post Office, 1910

A herd of cows amble past the Swan in this quiet 1910 scene.

Post Office, The Cross
— Staunton —

The Feathers Hotel, now demolished, in the centre of this 1910 photograph is fondly remembered by older residents for the dances held in its large room. Only the base of the high wall on the corner of Straight Lane now survives.

Staunton crossroads, *c.* 1905, with the Swan Hotel on the left and the post office on the right.

Several changes are apparent in this 1920 photograph of the Staunton Cross. There is now a pavement in front of the Swan, and a garage and petrol pumps fill the space beside the post office. A modern house and Ben Creese's butchers shop now occupy the site.

Left: Major reconstruction of St. Margaret's fourteenth-century spire took place in 1914. Four workmen pose on top of the scaffolding before replacing the top of the spire. Pub. anon. Posted 3 March 1914.

Below: James Houldey owned Corse Farm in Edwardian times when this photograph was taken. About this time the lime stucco on the overhanging gable was removed to reveal the old timbers. Pub. anon.

- FARMHOUSE -
- CORSE. GLOS. -

Twelve

Tibberton, Taynton and Barber's Bridge

The freedom of the road, in Tibberton, 1935.

Two teachers and twenty-four pupils of Taynton School pose for the camera in their Sunday best. Pub. anon.

Two little boys stroll safely along a traffic-free road, around 1935.

Rear view of the rectory with the rector's wife and some staff posing outside. Rabbits must have been a problem as the garden is surrounded by chicken wire.

Front view of Tibberton rectory, *c.* 1930 when Herbert Morris was the incumbent.

This memorial to Welsh soldiers killed in a battle in the civil war in 1643 had to be moved to accommodate the new bypass road round the old railway bridge. It was originally erected in 1871 by W.P. Price, M.P. for Gloucester City. Pub. Brooke, Gloucester.

Tibberton Church Sunday School was built in 1908 at a cost of £1,050. This photograph shows it just after completion with building materials still lying on the ground.

Barber's Bridge station lying derelict about 1968. Fortunately it was bought and renovated and is now the only remaining building on the Gloucester–Ledbury line. Photograph, D. White.

This is Barber's Bridge station viewed from the road bridge, c. 1920. The passing loop and down platform were taken out of use about 1898. The entrance to the goods yard can just be seen at the end of the platform. Pub. anon.

Thirteen

Upleadon

The forty-nine children and two teachers of Upleadon Schools, 7 May 1907.

This distinctive octagonal cottage on the crossroads was for many years the post office.

Several of these old water mills still survive on the River Leadon, like this one at Upleadon.
Pub. Citizen.

The attractive church of St. Mary, mainly twelfth century but with a rare half-timbered tower of c. 1500. The church was built on a clay bound which has caused constant concern over the centuries with expansion and shrinkage necessitating repairs.

Another view of the church, together with surrounding buildings, c. 1965.

Publishers of Newent Postcards

M.P. Bendle, Newsagent, Newent
W.H. Bendle, The Library, Newent
Berkley, Newent
C.M. Bisco , Newent
R.H. Bisco, Newent
A.G. Bidmead, Newent
B.M. Bidmead, The Stores, Newent
F.J. Brook, Printer, Gloucester
Clark, Printer, Newent
Gloucester Co-operative Society, Gloucester
W.G. Coles, Gloucester
I.M. Dyke, The Library, Newent
M.E.I. Jones, Newent
P.C. Lodge, The George, Newent
M.M. Martin, Postman, Newent
A.H. Pitcher, College Court, Gloucester
S.A. Pitcher, College Court, Gloucester
Smith, The Wool Shop, Newent
Stephens Brothers, Tibberton
The Good News Centre, Newent
The Shambles Museum, Newent
W.A. Call, County Studio, Monmouth
J.J. Tilley & Son, Ledbury
A.W.S. Tozer, Post Office, Redmarley
D. Bick, Pound House, Newent
Gloucestershire Federation of Womens Institutes

National Publishers include:

Airco Aerials Limited Hendon, London
D.V.P., Leicester
Excel
G. Hadfield, Liverpool
Judges, Hastings
R.A. Rapco (postcards), London
R. Tuck & Son, London
Wildt & Kray, London
Wright Tourist Products, Rugby
Young & Company